# THE BEST OF BRITISH

*hs*

# MORGAN

### KEN HILL

SUTTON PUBLISHING LIMITED

Sutton Publishing Limited
Phoenix Mill · Thrupp · Stroud
Gloucestershire · GL5 2BU

First published 1997

**British Library Cataloguing in Publication Data**
A catalogue record for this book is available from the
British Library.

ISBN 0-7509-1368-1

Typeset in 10/12 Perpetua.
Typesetting and origination by
Sutton Publishing Limited.
Printed in Great Britain by
Ebenezer Baylis, Worcester.

Sales were dependent on world records and in late 1912 HFS became engaged in a battle between himself and a GWK driven by J.T. Wood for the One Hour Record. The record attempts were held at Brooklands race track, and ended on Saturday 23 November when HFS made the record his by covering the distance shown in the advertisement and winning a special cup. (See page 114)

# CONTENTS

Introduction                                                    5

1.   The Founder & Family                                       7

2.   The Development of the Three-Wheeler Car                  25

3.   The Development of the Four-Wheeler Car                   45

4.   The Morgan Factory                                        65

5.   Morgan Personalities                                      81

6.   Advertising & Marketing                                   97

7.   Three Wheelers in Competition                           113

8.   Four Wheelers in Competition                            133

     Acknowledgements                                        160

# THE SPIRIT OF THE BIG RACING CAR!

## NEW WORLD'S RECORDS

set up by Mrs. G. M. Stewart and Mr. W. D. Hawkes on the Montlhery Track, August 6th :—

5 Kilos at 113·52 m.p.h. = 182·704 k.p.h.
5 Miles „ 107·51 „ = 173·026 „
10 Kilos (from standing start) at 102·72 m.p.h. = 165·319 k.p.h.
10 Miles at 102·81 m.p.h. = 165·456 k.p.h.

And at Arpajon on August 24th :—

FLYING KILO
at **115·6** m.p.h.
FLYING MILE
at **114·8** m.p.h.
(Subject to confirmation).

The MORGAN RUNABOUT Super-Sports Model at £150 is built to provide the exhilarating speed and power desired by the sportsman. It embodies a wealth of experience acquired at that great racing centre, Brooklands, and in important road events all over the world. The special O.H.V. engine will attain speeds up to 80 m.p.h. and can be tuned to considerably exceed this speed. Tax is only £4, and running and maintenance charges are proportionately low, giving total figures equivalent to those of the motorcycle and sidecar. The new MORGAN List giving particulars of all 1930 models may be had post free—write TO-DAY for a copy.

## The Morgan Runabout

MORGAN MOTOR CO., LTD.,
MALVERN LINK, WORCESTERSHIRE

Fantastic speed achieved by Mrs Gwenda Stewart in 1930 naturally warranted a full page advertisement in nearly every motorcycle magazine of the time.

# INTRODUCTION

The oldest one family motor manufacturer in the world is without doubt Morgan. At the age of twenty Henry Frederick Stanley Morgan ('HFS' as he was to become known throughout the motoring world), designed and built his first single-seater three-wheeled experimental car. At that time he could never have dreamt that within fifteen years he would become one of the world's major three-wheeler car manufacturers. Nor could he have envisaged that the company he founded would still be manufacturing sports cars eighty-eight years later. The success of his cars has always been dependent upon the phenomenal power to weight ratio: this has resulted in an amazing competition record achieved by both factory-entered and privately owned cars throughout the world.

The son of a country clergyman, HFS was lucky not to be forced to enter the Church as a profession. Far from discouraging him, his parents and grandparents gave him every assistance to make his own way in life. Educated at Stone House, Broadstairs and Marlborough College he then entered Crystal Palace Engineering College in South London, and it was here that his design and artistic talents developed. In 1906 he left the Great Western Railway, for which he had worked as a draughtsman, and went into partnership with a close friend; they opened a garage in Malvern, Worcestershire, and a few months later another in Fore Street, Worcester. The venture flourished and HFS was then able to turn his thoughts to making a car of his own design, a vehicle which would be a cross between a motorcycle and a car – not a motorcycle combination but a cyclecar.

The prototype was completed in 1909 and was a single-seater, fitted with tiller steering. It also incorporated Morgan's special form of independent front suspension. This form of sliding pillar front suspension is still used, with the addition of such refinements as rebound springs and shock absorbers, on the modern four-wheeler Morgan. The basic design is the same, but HFS was one of those very rare inventors who got the design right first time. The whole car was very light and was fitted with a 7 hp Peugeot motorcycle engine.

By November 1910 the Morgan Motor Company had been formed and the partners exhibited two different models, both single seaters, at the Motor Cycle Show at Olympia. The car attracted a lot of attention but few orders. Both men were disappointed, and Morgan's partner decided that the idea was too risky and withdrew. HFS decided to continue on his own, building a few cars to fulfil the orders that they had received. He realised that if he was to stay in business the car had to prove itself in competitions, and he had to design a two-seater model. His single seater was suitable for his own purposes and in competition but was not a commercial proposition.

1912 was to be a momentous year for HFS, with three major events taking place. This was the year that the Morgan Motor Company Limited was formed, and also made a small but significant profit of £1,314. It was also the year that he married Ruth Day, the daughter of a local vicar. She was to prove to be the added driving force behind HFS, giving advice and encouragement whenever necessary. Particularly in the early years she accompanied him on very many trials and competitions, acting as 'bouncer' on the steep hills. Somehow she still managed to have five children, four girls, and one son, Peter, who was to take over the company later.

On the death of his father in 1936 HFS, who was managing director of the company, succeeded him as chairman. A works manager, George Goodall, was appointed soon after and about eighteen months later was appointed managing director. This made for a far more relaxed life for HFS.

Continuing success in competition of all kinds meant that sales figures soared as did the profits. Sales were close to 1,000 cars in the year immediately before the war, and included export sales to France, Russia, India and North and South America. The post-war demand for motors by the public far outstripped supply, resulting in prices shooting up throughout the industry. Such was the demand that by 1923 Morgans were also being manufactured under licence by Darmont in France, the Darmont Morgan being virtually identical but fitted with a Blackburn engine. Lowering the prices, careful planning of the introduction of improvements, the loyalty of the workforce, who did not strike, and the continuing competition successes all served to ensure the survival of the company.

Peter Morgan was educated at Oundle School and in 1936 continued his education at the Chelsea College of Automobile Engineering, where he stayed until the outbreak of war when he enlisted in the Royal Army Service Corps and became a workshop officer. He was posted to Africa and ended up in charge of the Army workshop in Nairobi. He was released in 1946 having reached the rank of captain, and immediately joined the company, taking a seat on the Board of Directors. In 1958 George Goodall retired and Peter took over as managing director; the following year, on the death of his father, he became chairman. This meant that he had very little time to continue his highly successful competition driving. However he did return to trials competition for a short time, driving the prototype Plus 4 Plus model.

These changes coincided with a general slump in the world car market. It was obvious that if the company was to survive there had to be an all-out effort to increase production, sales and to reduce costs. To this end Peter Morgan called a meeting of the entire staff and explained the position, and with typical loyalty they responded to the challenge. The depression was particularly acute in America (Morgan's main export market), and this alone almost finished Morgan. However, three major events proved to be the company's saviour: Chris Lawrence's success in the 1962 Le Mans 24 Hour race, the resulting Plus 4 Super Sports model, and last but by no means least the introduction of the controversial Plus 4 Plus Fixed Head Coupé.

The development of the Plus 8 model and the acquisition of adjoining property in the late 1960s and early 1970s were achieved without recourse to outside funding. Sales continued to increase and by 1979 the delivery date for orders of about five years was the norm, and still applies today.

The late 1950s and early 1960s were also a time when Peter Morgan resisted a few tentative approaches for a take-over of the company by much larger motor manufacturers. Another lesson learnt was the need to ensure that never again would the company be dependent on one major export market.

Peter Morgan's son Charles was to carry on the family tradition of competition successes, becoming an excellent racing driver of Morgans (British Sports Car Champion in 1978 and 1979). Like his father Charles attended Oundle School, and obtained a BA (Hons) degree at Sussex University. He then took up a career as a TV cameraman, covering the trouble spots of the world. In 1984 he joined the company, and is now production director.

Such is the buoyant state of the company in recent years that it has not been necessary to advertise anywhere in the world since 1984.

# THE FOUNDER & FAMILY

*Henry Frederick Stanley Morgan (1881–1959): the
founder of the Morgan Motor Company Limited.*

H.F.S. Morgan as a young boy.

HFS, as he was to become known throughout the motor industry, *c.* 1912.

HFS's father, the Prebendary H. George Morgan, the first chairman of the company. He was completely dedicated to the company and it was not unknown for him to write (under a pseudonym) controversial letters to the motoring press, to stimulate public interest in the marque. Should this bring little or no response he would answer himself in a manner most likely to stimulate debate, using another pseudonym.

HFS's father, mother, and three sisters, Freida, Dorothy (the youngest), and Ethel.

HFS driving the first motor car he owned, an Eagle Tandem, seen here outside Stoke Lacy vicarage.

HFS developed his car using the facilities of Malvern College with the assistance of W. Stephenson-Peach, the engineering master at the college, who is seen here driving the single-seater prototype car. Note the tiller steering.

Public demand was for a two-seater car, which HFS quickly designed and built — but he retained the tiller steering. He is seen here with his future brother-in-law, William Cowpland.

'Fascinating, but very simple design.' A 1910 cartoon depicts the great interest shown in the Morgan single-seater prototype at the Olympia Motor Cycle Show.

Ruth Day, the daughter of the Reverend Archibald Day, vicar of St Matthias, Malvern Link, who became Mrs H.F.S. Morgan in June 1912.

HFS and Ruth leave on their honeymoon from the rectory of St Matthias. Immediately behind the car is Ruth's brother Geoffrey Day, a director of the company, and beyond him is HFS's father-in-law.

HFS and his sister Dorothy. Note that the tiller steering has now been changed to wheel.

In April 1914 a motoring rally was held at Great Malvern. Dorothy and her father are here directed to the parking area by an AA man.

The rally created a lot of interest, with a large turnout by both motorists and the public.

The Morgan family pose for a photograph outside the rectory at Stoke Lacy. Left to right: HFS and Ruth Morgan, Geoffrey Day and Dorothy, and Mr and Mrs Morgan senior. Geoffrey Day was believed to have been courting Dorothy at the time but was killed at Gallipoli during the First World War. Dorothy never married.

Another family photograph, c. 1915. In the foreground just left of centre is the experimental four wheeler which HFS designed. It was not until 1936, however, that such a car went into production.

HFS and Ruth with their first daughter, Sylvia. In all the family had four daughters, Sylvia, Stella, Brenda and Barbara (known as Bobbie), and one son, Peter.

The four-seater prototype, 1912/13. In this photograph, taken at Stoke Lacy, HFS and Ruth share the front seats, and sister Dorothy and Ruth's brother Geoffrey Day are the rear seat passengers.

Ruth Morgan in the road outside the rectory at Stoke Lacy. Although she drove and travelled thousands of miles with HFS in rallies, trials and so on, she did not drive competitively herself.

HFS was to own several other makes of motor car over the years. Here Ruth can be seen in a 1915 Prince Henry Vauxhall, and Dorothy in her Morgan.

Sylvia and Stella Morgan (HFS's sisters) seen above ready to play a round of golf, and below at the Auto Cycle Union Rally at Donington Park in 1934.

A collection of Morgan family cars in the late 1920s.

HFS's Rolls-Royce, the body of which was built at the Morgan factory. Note the Flying Stork mascot as supplied on Morgan cars rather than the usual Rolls-Royce Spirit of Ecstasy mascot.

A Morgan family outing with HFS's Rolls-Royce Phantom II in the lead.

Mrs Jane Morgan with Peter Morgan's works Drop Head Coupé on a caravanning holiday at Mableys Farm Field, Trebetherick, Cornwall, 1950.

Peter Morgan, the present managing director of the
Morgan Motor Company Limited.

Charles Morgan, director of the company, and son of Peter
Morgan.

Peter Morgan in the 1913 car which is normally kept on display at the Science Museum, when it was at the works for renovation.

Charles Morgan with a Plus 8 at St Moritz for the hundredth anniversary of the Cresta Run in 1985. The Sotheby's Cup races were part of the celebrations.

Peter Morgan, driving the prototype fuel injected Plus 8, prepares to drive off from outside the Morgan
factory in Pickersleigh Road, Malvern Link.

# DEVELOPMENT OF THE THREE-WHEELER CAR

*The twin-cylinder 1910 Olympia Show Car had an 8 hp engine and tiller steering. At this time Morgan offered a steering wheel for an extra charge.*

Not a Grand Prix model but a Sporting model (the driver sits on top of the bevel box), fitted with a 670 cc Blumfield engine. This vehicle was used by Vernon Busby in the BMCRC High Speed Reliability Trail on 29 March 1913, and was later given by HFS to his sister Dorothy.

R. James, the Sheffield Morgan agent, seen here in a Standard model, 1912.

Another example of the Standard model of 1912. By 1913 the tail-end of the body was enclosed.

A lovely example of an early Runabout.

This is an example of a 1912 De Luxe model. Note the central mounted Light Car AA badge, now most sought after by collectors.

The Commercial Carrier was based on the Standard model and introduced in 1913. The load container could be removed so that the vehicle could also be used as a passenger vehicle.

Mr Fry, son of the Bristol-based chocolate family, seen here in a 1913 Grand Prix model.

The 1914 Sporting model, which is on display at the London Science Museum.

The prototype of a Morgan developed for military use in the First World War. The back platform was designed for the mounting of a machine gun.

The car was also capable of carrying a driver and two passengers.

Two delightful studies of a little girl who is fascinated by the 1914/18 period Grand Prix model.

The Family model was to prove to be a very popular model. Here HFS and Ruth pose in the prototype car with borrowed children, complete with suitcase to show exactly how much room was available.

An early 1920s example of a Grand Prix model fitted with a side valve JAP engine. The extra passenger on the back was not illegal at that time, but not many people were brave enough to travel far in this position.

Another example of the early 1920s Grand Prix model, this one fitted with a MAG engine.

This Family model is fitted with a spring steel bumper, supplied by the factory as an optional extra.

A 1926 Aero model with water-cooled side valve JAP engine, and Ghost silencers. Note the youthful driver: in 1926 it was legal for a fourteen-year-old to ride motorcycles, and the Morgan was classified as a motorbike.

An Anzani-engined Aero model, 1927. This car has been fitted with non-standard sidelights.

The Aero model underwent many styling changes through its thirteen-year history. This 1924 model with water-cooled Blackburn engine has been given a number of non-standard modifications, including a fitted section between the two aero-screens and side-lights atop the front wings – never a production feature.

In October 1926 Morgan introduced the Aero Family model with the wheelbase extended by 4 inches to accommodate the two extra seats. It was powered by a JAP LTOW engine.

Two early van designs produced by the factory. The version above, without doors, is the earlier two-speeder, while that below is built on an R-type chassis with a JAP LTZ engine and a three-speed gearbox.

This Delivery vehicle is a 1929 model, exhibited at the 1927 Motor Cycle Show. The 'Box-Carrier' was built on a Family chassis but was not very convenient to use, having limited load space, accessed only from the top.

In 1933 the Newport, Monmouthshire police decided to replace their motorcycle and sidecar patrol vehicles with Family model Morgans. They are seen here taking delivery of them from Newport Morgan agent Alex Thom.

This specially bodied Super Sports shows the horizontal spare wheel mounting and the exhaust pipes lowered 6 inches in an effort to stop complaints from owners of burnt sleeves and elbows.

Morgan versatility: this 1934 JAP-engined Super Sports model was well able to cope with another two wheels and the weight of the boat and trailer.

The difficulties experienced by the factory over locating the spare wheel (this became available when they started to fit interchangeable wheels) was solved by modifying the rear of the Super Sports and inserting the wheel into the tail of the car. This was to become known as the 'Barrel Back'.

Morgan owners have always been a hardy breed. Come rain or snow and ice the majority have chosen to ride 'topless'. However the correct dress has always been necessary, as can be seen in this pre-Second World War photograph of a 1936 MX 2.

The post-war F Super model used the E93A Ford engine from the Ford 10. Production continued until 1952.

As early as 1915 HFS invented a system whereby the hood could be erected while the car was in motion. Here, thirty-five years later, the principle is demonstrated on an F4.

Three wheeler on test: Bruce Main-Smith of *Motor Cycling* magazine test-driving Ken Bayliss' 1949 F Super in 1956, four years after production of all three wheelers had ceased.

The F-type Ford engine was mounted in a 'Z' section chassis which in turn could easily be altered to make a four wheeler. This can be seen in this photograph of the prototype F model.

Every Morgan enthusiasts' dream: a very original and very complete Morgan in need of restoration, which was discovered by chance in the USA. This Family model was completely restored and has won many competitions since.

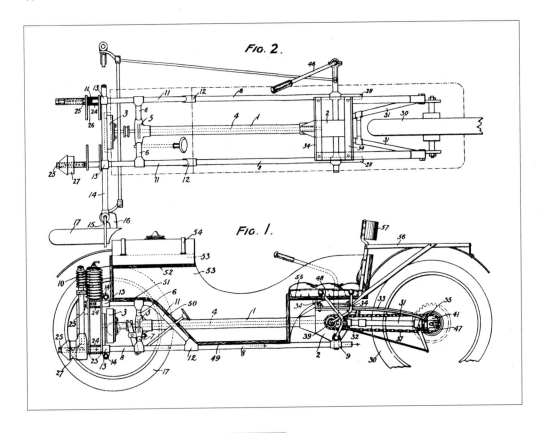

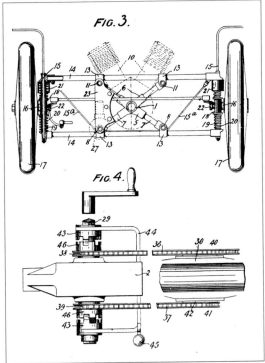

These are the patent drawings made in 1910 by John Black, a friend of HFS. He was to become Sir John Black, later the chairman of the Standard Motor Company. Standard produced a special engine for Morgans from 1938 to 1951.

# DEVELOPMENT OF THE FOUR WHEELER CAR

*The experimental four-wheeled Morgan was based on a F-type three-wheeler chassis (see previous chapter).*

The roadgoing version of the prototype four wheeler underwent extensive road trials in the summer of 1935.

After the success of the two-seater car a four-seater was introduced in August 1937. This is a beautifully restored example.

The four-wheeled Morgan proved to be a good export car and this one was exported direct to Holland.

The difference between the two rare Le Mans and TT Replica models can clearly be seen by comparing these two photographs. On the Le Mans the single spare wheel is mounted into the rear panel and on the TT it is mounted on the panel. There was no mechanical difference between the two models.

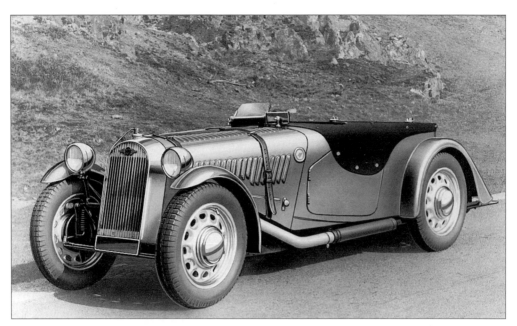

The production version of the Le Mans Replica, as illustrated here in a pre-production advertising postcard, can be seen to differ greatly from the author's car, shown on the previous page. Because of the outbreak of the Second World War this model was never to go into production, whereas the author's car was specially bodied originally for works use.

The instrumentation of the Morgan 4/4 was compact and easily readable by the driver.

Another popular model of the 4/4 was the Drop Head Coupé. Above is the experimental car made by the Avon Carriage Company, used by HFS as his personal car for nearly two years. In the photograph below it can be seen that not all the features of the experimental car were adopted for the production model.

After the war there was an acute shortage of sheet steel, so many cars were sold from the works in chassis form. These were bodied and panelled by outside companies in aluminium, and this resulted in some unusual body shapes being built.

The saloon version of the early Plus 4 is the only one of its type in the world, and was produced by Coopers Bodies of Putney.

Peter Morgan's personal Plus 4 Drop Head Coupé gained a silver award in the 1954 Exeter Trial, when it was driven by Peter Garnier and Charles Heywood of *The Autocar* magazine.

This Vanguard-engined two-seater Drop Head Coupé was originally built as a flat radiator model and left the works in August 1954. Having languished at a main agent's for a year, it was returned to the works to be rebodied with a cowled radiator and re-sold to another agent, leaving the factory in October 1955. Several of the final flat radiator cars were rebodied in this way.

The introduction of the 'interim radiator' model Plus 4 was forced upon the company by diminishing supplies of the integral radiators and free-standing headlamps. Above is a high lamp version, required to meet the new UK lighting regulations introduced in 1954. Below is an early example of a low lamp version, which has been successfully used in competition for many years by John Lindsey. Most of these cars were partially completed when the regulations changed, so they were finished as left-hand drive and exported.

With the curved grille and stoneguard the transition from flat to cowled radiator was complete. Initially the twin upright spare wheels were retained.

The competition version of the Series II 4/4 was introduced in September 1957, and was fitted with this Aquaplane aluminium alloy cylinder head and inlet manifold for improved performance.

This is the prototype of the 4/4 Series III, which was introduced in October 1960. It is seen here at the factory with, left to right, Joe Huxham (Bournemouth Morgan agent), W.A.G. (Jim) Goodall (works manager) and Peter Morgan.

A 1967 Series IV 4/4 with the interesting chassis number B690 was found under a pile of rubble in a contractor's yard in Nigeria. It has been fully restored and is now owned by the President of the Nigeria Motor Sports Club.

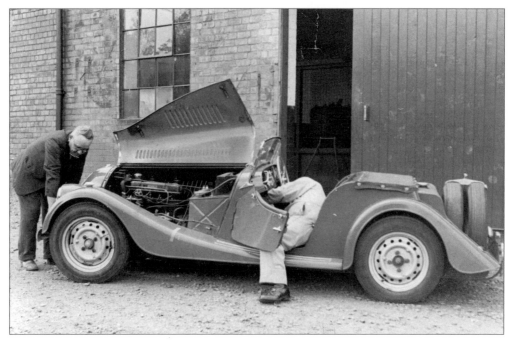

Charlie Curtis, the works chief tester until he retired in the early 1970s, is seen here preparing Peter Morgan's early TR2-engined Plus 4 rally car, KUY 387, for a rally. Note the white tape on the wings. This was placed there as an indicator to help the driver to stop astride lines, which was quite usual in rally tests of those days.

The cowled radiator four-seater Drop Head Coupé is seen here with hood and side screens erected. This model was not produced in great numbers, but is now regarded as a very desirable model.

The Lawrencetune hardtop, which was designed and developed by Chris Lawrence, was made initially to fit the low line Plus 4 models, although it could also be used for the 4/4 when supplied with different fittings. Moulded in resin-bonded glass-fibre, it was normally supplied white with a flock-sprayed inner finish, and it weighed 22 pounds.

The 1963 Plus 4 was fitted with a TR4 engine, which had twin SU carburettors fitted as standard. However, twin Stromberg carburettors were available as a factory option.

To date the only fully enclosed production Morgan has been the Plus 4 Plus Fixed Head Coupé. It had a very distinctive styling and was not well received at the time; only twenty-six were ever made. It is now a much sought-after collector's car.

The wooden former for the Plus 4 Plus Fixed Head Coupé, shown here arriving at E.B. Plastics. Here it was panelled in aluminium to make the mould for the glass-fibre body shells.

The Plus 4 Super Sports model was developed from the 1962 Le Mans car. The immediate recognition point of this model is the air intake on the side of the bonnet, which houses the twin Weber carburettors.

The TR4 and TR4A engines used in the Plus 4 Super Sports were tuned by Chris Lawrence. The conversion consisted of stripping the engine, balancing all moving parts, polishing and gas flowing the cylinder head and fitting a modified inlet manifold with a pair of Weber carburettors.

The 4/4 Series V Competition model used the Ford Cortina GT engine with a single choke Weber carburettor. Several owners undertook further modifications, like adding twin Webers, as shown here, in the quest for more power.

In 1968 the 4/4 Ford 1600 model was introduced. It was fitted with the Cortina engine which had increased displacement over the previous model. This is a four-seater version with all the weather equipment erected.

The prototype Plus 8 had two bulges in the bonnet to allow room for the dashpots of the SU carburettors. Note the wire spoked wheels; only three cars were fitted with these before they were introduced as an optional extra in 1993. Before the model went into production a completely new wheel was necessary to handle the torque generated by the V8 engine.

Another unique Morgan is this automatic transmission Plus 8 Drop Head Coupé which was built as an experiment. After extensive testing it was decided not to put the car into production, because of potential limited demand and because the extra weight affected performance. The car since then has been used by Mrs Jane Morgan as her personal transport.

This press release photograph of 1983 was entitled 'Fifty Years of Ford Power for Morgans'. 'Back in 1933, the new Morgan F4 three-wheeled sports car (front, left) was powered by the 933 cc engine of the Model Y Ford (back, right). Today the latest Morgan 4/4 (front, right) has the 1.6 litre CVH engine of the Ford XR3.'

The prototype fuel-injected Plus 8 outside the Morgan factory.

Morgan is the first independent sports car manufacturer in the UK to offer airbag protection as an optional extra. This was developed in conjunction with the Motor Industry Research Association Crash Protection Centre. In addition to the head and chest bag, knee bolsters help reduce leg injury. The bags became available for all models from 1997.

This publicity photograph issued to the motoring press for the launch of the Rover-engined Plus 4 in 1988 was staged in the factory yard with the aid of one or two props. The stained glass window above the door was presented to Peter Morgan by the Plus 4 Club of California to mark the seventy-fifth anniversary of the company in 1984.

New Morgans, lined up in the finishing and dispatching bay at the works, await collection by the eager owners.

# THE MORGAN FACTORY

*The Morgan Motor Company Factory at Worcester Road, Malvern Link, November 1913. The employees pose outside Chestnut Villa. HFS and Ruth's home is on the right.*

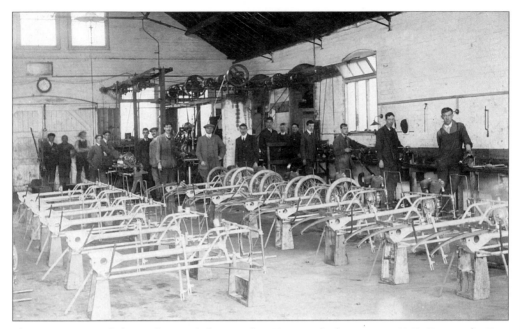

The Worcester Road chassis shop work-force with HFS in cap back centre, *c.* 1912. During the First World War the factory was made over to the production of shells and other munitions for the war effort. To avoid profiteering from the government contracts, a fixed profit allowance – generous by any standard – was legislated. The government also supplied or helped substantially with the cost of new machinery.

Car sales, particularly of open cars, was very seasonal in the 1920s and 1930s. During the winter few cars were sold, so the factory completed as many bodies and chassis as possible and placed them in temporary storage. Then all that was necessary was to fit the completed bodies to the completed chassis and the cars were ready for sale. In this way the factory was kept in production throughout the year. This photograph was taken during the winter of 1921/22.

The frame shop, with the brick hearths where the brazing of the chassis was carried out, *c.* 1927. These hearths are still in use today, with the front frames of all modern Morgans being brazed together by hand.

The machine shop as it was in the 1970s. Compare this with the photograph on page 66 (top), where all the overhead drive-shafts and uncovered drive belts came from the roof to the various machines. What the present-day factories inspector would have said about them does not bear thinking about. In fact HFS slipped on a spot of grease while walking through the machine shop in April 1919; instinctively he put out his right hand to save himself and it caught in the machinery. As a result the first two fingers of his right hand had to be amputated.

As post-war demand for the Runabout increased it soon became obvious that the Worcester Road factory was fast becoming too small. HFS therefore purchased a new site in Pickersleigh Road

and this opened on 16 October 1919. This photograph dates from about 1927.

The erecting shop. Throughout its long history the Morgan has never been built by mass production methods. The closest there has ever been is this shop. Here the chassis are laid out on trestles and then the various components are placed around them ready for fitting. As can be seen nothing much has changed over the last seventy years. However, in 1997 a completely new layout has been adopted. It was in this shop that Peter Morgan started work in the factory on 1 February 1947 after being demobbed from the Army.

The process nowadays is slightly different but in the days of the three wheelers the cars left this shop as a complete Morgan in chassis form. In these photographs the light-coloured chassis has a galvanised finish which is available as an optional extra. The Plus 8 engines and transmission are stored on the delivery pallets at one end of the shop and moved into position when needed by a hand-operated electric gantry crane which runs the whole length of the shop. However, in 1997 many changes have been introduced and now the chassis shop completes a predetermined daily batch.

The body shop. The wooden parts of the Morgan are milled and then assembled into a complete body frame. In the 1920s polar wood was used but now ash is preferred.

The sheet metal shop. Here the various body parts are cut and shaped to fit the wooden frame. Each panel is made to fit one frame only, and although apparently all the same, they do in fact differ and cannot be used on another body frame. In the 1927 photograph the gentleman in the centre wearing a bowler hat is the foreman Mr Sambrook. In the later photograph the gentleman in the centre is the then (1971) foreman Mr Sambrook junior. Between them they spent over fifty years working at the factory.

Today the sheet metal shop still looks the same, except for the model of Morgan under construction. On 25 September 1997 the workforce will celebrate the diamond jubilee of their being placed on a five-day week for the first time, which incidentally coincided with the introduction of the four-seater 4-4 model. However, as from 1997, all this has changed. Now there are no more rolling chassis in the sheet metal shop.

The paint shop. The mottled dashboard of the Family model in the foreground of the 1929/30 photograph was introduced in 1928. On the left, halfway down the workshop, is a Delivery Van. All painting at this time was carried out by hand and brush (coachpainting). Note the brushes in the foreground. Later a combination of spraying and brush painting was introduced. Now the process is all machine spraying and baking, but the process of rubbing down between coats is still carried out by hand. Water-based paints are now used, as from 1997.

The trim shop. Here the upholstery, hoods and tonneau covers are tailored to each individual vehicle. Note the rolls of various carpeting, etc., mounted on the rack in the centre of the workshop.

The dispatch and delivery bay. A selection of flat radiator Morgans await delivery, c. 1950. There is a selection of two and four-seaters plus Drop Head Coupés. In this bay the cars are checked and polished and minor defects, if any, are dealt with before they are dispatched to the various agents world wide.

To visit the Morgan factory is to step back in time. If anyone from the early days of the Pickersleigh Road factory should enter the stores and offices he would immediately recognise the area. There may now be a few more storage racks and the contents are different, but the floor, office doors and other items remain the same as they were seventy-five years ago. However, hidden behind a filing case there is a photocopying machine which they would not recognise.

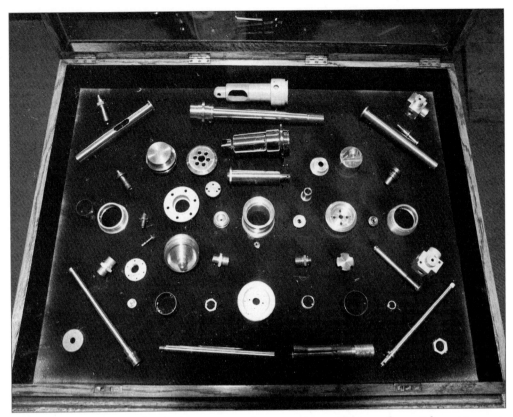

During the Second World War the factory was made over to the manufacture of essential precision parts for the Oerlikon gun and various hydraulic undercarriage components, gauges and compressor parts for aircraft. No cars were produced during this period.

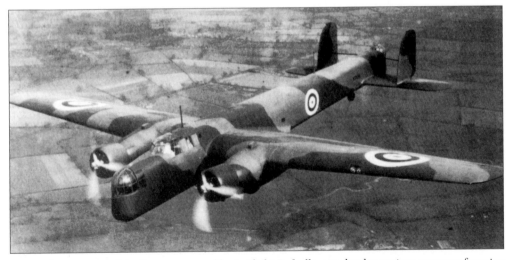

During the war, part of the factory was used by In Flight Refuelling to develop various measures for wing de-icing. A Whitney bomber like this was assembled in some of the workshops so that various devices could be developed and then tested on aircraft in flight.

The works clock, which for years was used by employees to clock in and out of the factory.

The original Worcester Road factory as it was in the 1970s and 1980s. On the right can be seen the house in which Peter Morgan was born.

The dispatch bay as it is today. A mixture of Plus 8s, Plus 4s and 4/4s await their eager new owners, who placed their order for the car five or six years ago. One receives a final polish.

# MORGAN PERSONALITIES

*Captain Albert Ball, RFC, VC, DSO, MC in his MAG-engined Grand Prix Morgan. He was credited with shooting down over forty German aeroplanes in the First World War. In May 1917 he was a member of No. 56 Squadron which was equipped with the then new SE5 fighter aircraft, which fought the world's first mass air-battle. The squadron had been specifically formed to outfly and outfight the famous 'Red Baron', Baron Von Richthofen and his brother with their 'Circus', as his squadron was known. The 'Circus' outnumbered the British by more than two to one, and with greater power slowly overpowered the British. They were forced to scatter and Captain Ball was last seen disappearing into a cloud bank during the dog fight. No trace was found of his aircraft.*

Miss Dorothy Morgan, the youngest sister of HFS, seen here in the car which HFS gave her as a birthday present. She was to live to a grand old age and presented the prizes at the seventy-fifth anniversary celebrations, where she was the guest of honour.

The coachpainters take a lunch break at the Pickersleigh Road factory, c. 1922. The young apprentice (centre back row) is W.G. Phillips.

The Morgan Motors football team were league champions in 1920/21. HFS is seated second from right in the front row. Other members of the team were M. Chiddy, B. Berry, E. Pyler, F. Foulkes, D. Hawker, Mr Morris, P. Corbett, B. Galfield, Mr Dobbs, Mr Hales, B. Gulliver, E. Stanley and J. Sambrook.

One of the most famous of all the Morgan competition drivers in the early days of the company was E.B. Ware, the head of the research department of JAP Engines. He is seen here with his racing mechanic immediately after winning the Junior Car Club General Efficiency Trial in a Morgan Runabout in 1923.

The Bournemouth Rally, 1925. HFS is at the wheel and Ruth keeps cool under a parasol.

Harold Beart in his Blackburne-engined Morgan, 1926.

Robin Jackson in his record-breaking, Blackburne-engined lightweight aluminium Morgan Special. He is seen here before he romped home, an easy winner of the New Cycle Car Club three-lap Handicap race at Brooklands in August 1928.

Mr and Mrs Clive Lones, who together had won the New Cycle Car Club 50-mile Cyclecar Grand Prix at Brooklands in August 1928.

Mrs Lones is congratulated by HFS at the prize-giving after the Cyclecar Grand Prix. The small boy in the school cap is Peter Morgan.

George Goodall, works manager of the Morgan Motor Company, was known as 'Uncle George'. Here he is having fun on a Brough Superior 11-50 at Brooklands in 1935.

Mrs Gwenda Stewart, who broke numerous world records in her specially prepared 750 and 1100 cc JAP-engined Morgans. In 1929 she achieved 101.55 miles in one hour. This was the first time that 100 miles had been covered in an hour by any three wheeler. To put this into perspective the motorcycle and sidecar record stood at 89.4 miles an hour.

Another study of Gwenda Stewart, after she had achieved a 5 km record of 113.52 mph. In all she broke fifty-seven records in 1930. The inscription reads 'To Mr Morgan in gratitude and appreciation for his having made a "thoroughbred" which at all times was a joy to handle.'

This composite photograph, taken from an early owner's manual, was entitled 'Personalities behind the Morgan'.

Joe Huxham, the Bournemouth Morgan agent, is seen here with his MX2 Sports Model Morgan fitted with regulation fishtail silencers at the 1934 Brooklands Races. He was a member of the West Hampshire Light Car Club Team. The works pick-up truck can be seen in the background.

George Goodall with his son W.A. (Jim) Goodall, who won a Premier Award and First in Class in the 1938 RAC Rally.

Prudence Fawcett in the car she drove to and competed in in the 1938 Le Mans 24 Hour race. This was her first race, the regulations being a little more flexible in those days.

Geoffrey White, who had been Prudence Fawcett's co-driver in 1938, teams up with Dick Anthony for the 1939 Le Mans 24 Hour race.

Rob Laurie was an experienced Le Mans competitor who often entered his own cars: in 1949 an Aston Martin, in 1950 a Riley and in 1951 a Jaguar XK120. In 1952 he entered the race with a Plus 4 supplied by the Morgan Motor Company. This car was not new and had been used in numerous rallies and trials. He was forced to retire after about six hours when a valve and piston made contact.

Chris Lawrence competed in the 1962 Le Mans in his Plus 4 Morgan TOK 258, and was also very successful in other races, as was his friend Robin Grey in his specially prepared Morgan. They are seen here outside the Lawrencetune Works with just a few trophies they had won.

Above: Peter Morgan and Ray Meredith receiving a trophy after success in the MCC National Rally in November 1956. Below, from left to right: Ray Meredith, Tommy Thompson, Les Yarranton (receiving the tankard), Jim Goodall, and Peter Morgan receiving the Team Award trophies in the same event.

The works staff pose for a group photograph, March 1968. Peter Morgan is in the foreground, right.

The factory workforce pose for another group photograph. Behind the wheel is Charlie Curtis, who was the works chief tester from 1947 to 1971.

Maurice Owen and his assistant Chris at work on the experimental Plus 8 in the development department at the factory. Note the twin SU carburettor dash pots, which caused the bonnet of the prototype to have two bumps in the top.

Dick Pritchard, the first chairman of the Morgan 4/4 Club, preparing for a commemorative run up Prescott Hill during the sixtieth anniversary celebrations of the Morgan Motor Company in 1970. This was the last time he actually drove his 1939 4/4 Le Mans. He then gave the car to his niece and nephew (the author and his wife) who still own the car.

# ADVERTISING & MARKETING

*As can be seen from this advertisement, HFS entered the first London to Exeter Trial and won his first gold medal. This was to be the first of hundreds of competitive events that he would enter over the years. By the time the 1911 Motor Cycle Show was held in November he had developed the two-seater model, and after the show he found himself overwhelmed with orders. To maintain this interest he and his cars had to continue to be successful in competition.*

# The Speediest Cyclecar in the World Beats every other Competitor in the
# GRAND PRIX
## The famous British
# MORGAN

—driven by Mr. W. G. McMinnies, a British driver—won the race at an average speed of 42 miles an hour, in spite of a certain amount of bad luck. Starting fourth, it was not long before Mr. McMinnies forged his way into the leading position. But he was not to hold it for long. Tyre trouble delayed him, and he started again to find that he had dropped from first to fifteenth place. The Morgan was asked to accomplish what looked like a hopeless task—and not in vain. The temporary leaders were overhauled, one by one, until Mr. McMinnies, though hampered by another delay, had recaptured the place of honour and romped home an easy winner.

We can supply exactly similar machines for £115, particulars on application. :: Other patterns from 85 Guineas. ::

Cyclecar Club Hill Climb at South Harting:
Class I.   Mr. A. W. Lambert, Silver Plaque.
Class IV.  Mr. W. G. McMinnies, 1st on Time and Formula. Silver Plaque.
            Mr. A. W. Lambert, 2nd on Time and Formula, Bronze Medal.

## MORGAN MOTOR CO., LTD.,
### MALVERN.

B3

The Cycle Car Grand Prix success mentioned in the advertisement was the cause for the overwhelming demand for HFS's cars.

With huge numbers of the male population away at war all manufacturers seized on the idea of using servicemen to add appeal to their advertisements.

One of the last competitions held before war was declared on 3 August 1914 was this trial. The driver of the car illustrated was Mr James, the Morgan agent in Sheffield.

The photograph reproduced above shows the

**WINNER OF THE OPEN CYCLECAR CLASS** in the Essex Motor Club's Hill Climb at Kop Hill, Saturday, 14th March, 1914.

*Other recent successes are as follow*
CYCLECAR CLUB TRIAL —— SECOND.
1st and 3rd — Acceleration ;     1st — Hill Climbing and Re-starting ;
3rd — Starting Engine ;     2nd and 3rd — Brooklands Test Hill ;     2nd
and 3rd — Two Morgans equal — Petrol Consumption.
COLMORE CUP TRIAL. Special Prize for Best Cyclecar.

Morgan Motor Co., Ltd., Malvern Link.

*Morgan Runabout*

Success in competition sold cars. Almost every new Morgan advertisement featured yet another success from the previous week.

*The* Morgan Runabout

Has the comfort of a CAR and the economy of the MOTOR CYCLE.

**It affords good protection in all weathers.**

Motor Cycle Show, Olympia, Stand 53.

MORGAN MOTOR CO., LTD.,     MALVERN LINK.

There were the occasional exceptions to the rule, but even then a Morgan in competition is used within the advertisement.

Few cyclecars could even begin to scale hills of the gradient shown in this advertisement.

When the post-war depression was at its height Morgan interspersed the 'success' advertisements with those emphasising the 'family' and 'economy' advantages of owning a Morgan.

With the increase of petrol prices in the spring of 1929, the economy of the Morgan became even more important as a selling point.

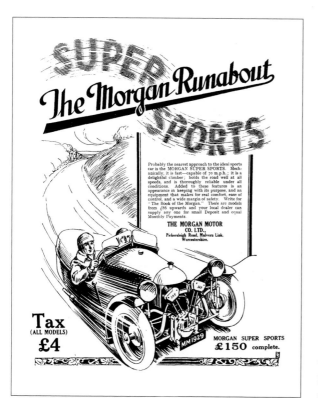

There were still those prospective buyers who were searching for speed and stamina.

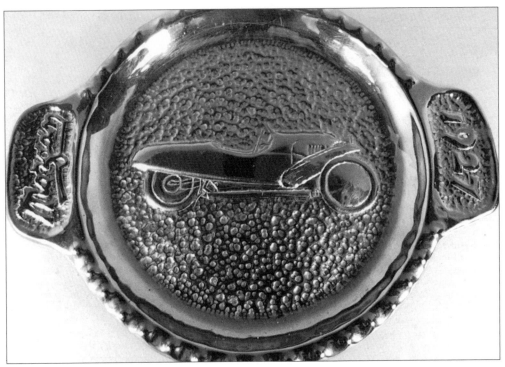

The 6.75 inch diameter tray advertising the Aero model was produced by the factory in 1927, and was circulated to their main agents.

About the same period the factory also issued these bakelite inkwells to their agents and outlets.

The Family model had been one of the mainstays of the factory production throughout the 1920s and 1930s. It was therefore only natural that the surrounding countryside was used to illustrate their advertisements. Here a family pose with the F4 model against the backdrop of the Malvern Hills.

The introduction of cheap mass-produced four-wheeler cars in Britain in the late 1920s was to cause a complete change of direction in Morgan advertising. Economy, petrol consumption, and low tax were now the selling features. Slowly through the 1930s one by one the other manufacturers of three wheelers went out of business. The wording of this 1938 advertisement means exactly what it says.

The first important four-wheeler Morgan race result occurred in June 1937, when Belfast mechanic Robert Campbell became the surprise winner of the Ulster Trophy in a car owned by his employer's wife Mrs R.E. Parish. Campbell's chance to race came because his boss's competition licence had failed to come through in time.

Morgan again jumped to use the competition success of Miss Prudence Fawcett when she took part in the 1938 Le Mans 24 Hour race.

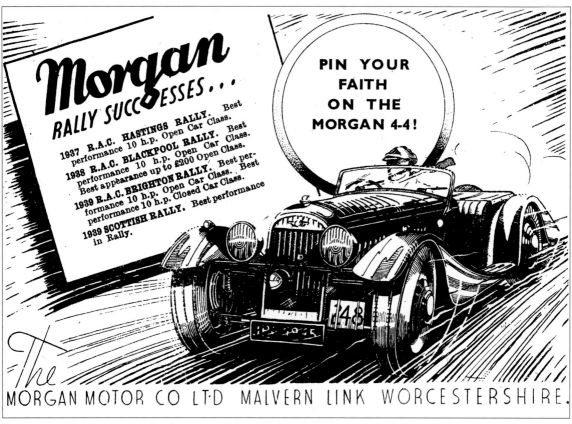

The new four-wheeler model was proving to be just as successful in competition as its three-wheeler predecessors, and Morgan lost no time in letting the public know about it.

This 1940 advertisement was couched in hopeful terms, but in actual fact by this time the whole factory had been made over to the making of aircraft parts and other items to help the war effort.

Unlike today Morgans were not sold before they were even manufactured and most agents at home and abroad carried a stock of new cars for immediate delivery. This photograph illustrates Morgan 4/4s fitted with the Standard Special engine, built in about 1949/50.

Originally introduced in November 1938, the Drop Head Coupé model was to prove very popular. In all sixty-one including the prototype were produced before the outbreak of the Second World War. Although this does not appear to be a very large number it does represent nearly a quarter of the four-wheeler Morgans produced during that period.

The Drop Head Coupé continued to be very popular after the war, and in the 1950s, with more power produced by the 2077 cc Standard Vanguard engine, even more so.

The 'transitional' style Plus 4 was neither a true 'upright' or 'flat' radiator model, which had been made since 1936, or the 'cowled' radiator that we know today. This model was manufactured for less than a year in small numbers; few of these cars still survive.

The Series II 4/4 model fitted with a Ford 10 hp engine was rather a mundane car for which outside companies produced tuning kits to sell to owners. Morgan soon realised there was a market for a competition version of the model and in November 1957 were producing them alongside the standard model.

The performance of the new Plus 4 was far superior to the 4/4, and the Morgan factory was quick to point this feature out to the public.

The Plus 4 Plus model was a complete departure from traditional Morgan styling and was greeted with mixed emotions by the motoring public and press. Only twenty-six were ever produced. It is interesting to note that Peter Morgan's daughter Lady Jane Colwyn posed with the prototype Plus 4 Plus model in all advertisements for it.

This advertisement was a complete departure from anything previously used by the Morgan company. Over the years many stars of stage, screen, radio, television and the pop music world have owned Morgans. However, this was the first instance that one of them had been used and named in one of the company's advertisements. It was also the first time that a simple illustration of a model had been coupled with clever simple wording.

Morgan Plus 8 with Hywell Bennett and Sue Lloyd, stars of Anglo-E.M.I. production 'Percy'.

The trend continued right up to 1984 when it became completely unnecessary for the company to advertise, owing to the huge waiting list for their cars – which is currently five to six years.

In 1996 the British Post Office produced a set of postage stamps depicting various famous makes of British motor cars. The highest value stamp depicted the front of a Plus 4 Morgan flat radiator Drop Head Coupé. Here Roger Pilkington poses with an enlarged publicity version of the stamp with his car on the old Brooklands Racetrack banking, with the members' bridge in the background. This bridge was used for the public to cross from the outside to the inside of the race track.

# THREE WHEELERS IN COMPETITION

*This is the very first competition appearance of a Morgan, with HFS driving his single-seater with tiller steering in the first London to Exeter Trial on Boxing Day, 1910. The problem for organisers of competitive motoring events at this time was exactly where a Morgan fitted, in the motorcycle or car category. It was some time before the Auto Cycle Union (ACU) and the RAC agreed that it should be classed as a motorcycle. Here a lonely Morgan awaits the start of a rally.*

HFS prepares for his world record breaking run at Brooklands in 1912. Beside HFS is his father, H.G. Morgan, in the top hat. The pipe smoker is A.V. Ebblewhite, the official Brooklands time keeper, and beside and to the back of him can just be seen Ruth Morgan.

The special trophy commissioned by *Motor Cycling* and *Cyclecar* magazines for the person who at the end of each year held the cyclecar one hour record.

HFS at speed on the banking during his record breaking hour run, when he finished just a few yards short of 60 miles within the hour.

The Scottish Trial in 1913 took competitors to some wild and lonely places. Here N.J. Brunell in his Morgan tackles Applecuss Hill.

HFS and Ruth at the start of the ACU Six Day Trial in August 1913. He won a gold award.

The motor car was still a rarity in 1913, and huge crowds gathered whenever a rally started. This one in May 1913 was no exception. The winning car was a Morgan which won the Wilson-Phillips Trophy.

The Hereford Automobile Club's Reliability Trial in 1913 also collected a crowd.

At times the trials route could be a lonely place. Here HFS and Ruth participate in a pre-First World War rally.

Morgans had a tendency to tilt over on hairpin bends, particularly on steep gradients. HFS and many other Morgan drivers had one hand gloved to help push themselves upright again. This Morgan came to grief on the 'Cornish Cliffs' rally.

E.B. Ware is seen here after his victory in the Light Car Long Handicap race at Brooklands in May 1920.

Lieutenant R.T. Messeroy and HFS nearing the summit of the 1 in 3 Old Wyche cutting in the Birmingham Trial of 1914.

Bill James, the son of Sheffield Morgan agent Billie James, takes to the water in the 1920 Six Day Trial.

HFS and Ruth keep close over to their right in an effort to find the smoothest possible route during a trial in 1919.

The Morgan team at Brooklands during the 1921 ACU Six Day Trial: HFS and Ruth (90), Frank Boddington (91) and Billy Elces (92).

E.B. Ware checks his race car before the start of the 200-mile race at Brooklands on 20 September 1924. Both Ware and his passenger Mr Alchin were severely injured when their car suddenly swerved, hit a fence and spun several times across the track; then they were thrown out of the car. So badly injured were they that they spent many months in hospital before they recovered enough to leave. Ware was never to race again.

Freddie James in a four-speed MAG-engined Morgan in the 1920 ACU Six Day Trial. The normal gearbox had only two speeds, but this car was fitted with another two-speed gearbox behind the clutch for trials purposes.

Another view of the 1 in 3 Old Wyche Cutting. Here a Grand Prix model fitted with a water-cooled MAG engine makes the climb in 1923.

HFS and Ruth set off after a lunch stop in the Motor Cycle Club 1000-mile Stock Machine Trial in 1924. In this type of trial the organisers would visit completely unannounced any one of the manufacturer's agents or factory and select any car from stock. This car was then fitted with seals and no preparation work could be carried out on it before the trial actually started. After this only normal maintenance was allowed.

ACU Six Day Trial, 1922: HFS was one of the three Morgans that won gold awards.

George Goodall driving an Aero model fitted with a 1096 cc overhead valve JAP engine. Here he is seen tackling Nunnery Lane during the 1928 ACU Six Day Stock Machine Trial.

Freddie James climbs Park Rash in his Family Aero during the 1928 International Six Day Trial.

Clive Lones (with his wife as passenger) rounds one of the Brooklands sand bank chicanes on his way to winning the New Cycle Car Club's Grand Prix, 30 August 1928.

S.A. Keay with passenger Al Slinger just clear the sand bank chicane in the same race.

Freddie James, seen here on Ilkley Moor, won a silver medal with his Family Aero in the 1928 International Six Day Trial.

John Fell with passenger P.C. Cliff participating in the Intervarsity Speed Trail at Copsall Park on 4 March 1933.

H.E. Glover-Fox's passenger moves his weight over to help stabilise the Morgan as it takes a right-hand bend, in a race organised by the MCC at Donington in June 1938.

It did not take long for motor racing to restart after the war. This line up at Cadwell Park on Easter Monday 1946 includes W. Spence (26, 596 cc Norton), John Surtees (42, 596 cc Norton) and C.S. Fairburn (67, Morgan).

This Morgan-based single-seater special is seen here competing at Madresfield in 1953.

John Bone in his 1938 'F' Super leaves the start at the Madresfield Speed Trials in 1953.

Gentle competition. Captain N.J. Clift RN of Winkleigh, Devon, takes the oldest known running Morgan, dating from 1912/13, up Prescott hill climb at a Vintage Sports Car Club meeting.

Fast and furious, as David Shotton with his passenger Mike Duncan negotiates a left-hand bend at Prescott in 1970. The car is powered by a Matchless engine.

Morgan three wheelers went out of production but not out of fashion. In this three-wheeler race in 1957 Ken Baylis in his F type mixes it with motorcycle combinations.

There is no stopping three-wheeler Morgans. In
1994 Hedwig Rodyns of Belgium entered the
Classic Monte Carlo Rally and was placed third
in his class in his F Super. On the second night
of the rally at the stopover it snowed heavily
with 10 inches lying on the countryside by the
time they set off on the next stage of the rally at
7.02 in the morning. Undaunted he and his
navigator Michael Munks did the whole rally
with the hood down.

# FOUR WHEELERS IN COMPETITION

*One of the two early 4-4s which did so well in the Irish Leinster Trophy and Ulster Trophy races in the summer of 1937.*

Miss Prudence Fawcett in the specially prepared 4-4 which in her first race in the 24 Hour Le Mans was placed second in her class and classed fourteenth overall in the Index of Performance. Her co-driver was Geoffrey White. Their average speed for the twenty-four hours was 57.2 mph and they covered a distance of 1,372.98 miles. This car was actually driven to the event by Miss Fawcett and home after it.

The RAC Blackpool Rally of 1938 in which Miss D.L. Bean won a Premier Award and also was placed first in the coachwork competition. The Morgan beside her is that of George and Jim Goodall who won their class and a Premier Award.

This 1936 4-4 was exported direct to Australia where it was extensively raced before being rebodied after an accident. The single-seater body was built from chicken wire and papier maché. It is seen here with its then owner Jim Boughton on 10 April 1939 at the 150 mile race at Bathurst, Australia. The car still survives today and is now owned by Craig Schubert.

H.F.S. Morgan drives his personal Drop Head Coupé to a class win and a Premier Award in the 1939 RAC Brighton Rally.

George Goodall completes the kerb test at Pitlochry in the eighth RSAC Scottish Rally in May 1939. He finished first overall.

Peter Morgan at speed at Silverstone on 20 April 1949 in the TT Replica 4-4.

The prototype Plus 4 takes a corner in wet weather at the Prescott Hill climb.

Two views of Peter Morgan negotiating an artificial chicane during the manoeuvrability tests on the sea front at Bournemouth during the 1951 RAC Rally in the Plus 4 Drop Head Coupé. But for a slight error of judgement on this test he could well have beaten the might of the Jaguar XK120 works team. He was leading up to the final test and lost by just 2.15 marks.

In Chris Lawrence's first full season of racing in 1957 he was to win nine marque races and a handicap race. He also came second four times and third once, and finished in every race. Here he leads the field in the BRSCC Brands Hatch marque race meeting on 10 May, where he achieved his first marque win in a Morgan.

Chris Lawrence laps an MG on his way to victory in the BARC marque race at Goodwood, 27 July 1959.

In 1961 Pip Arnold competed in the Coppa Inter-Europa race at Monza in XRX 1, which was fitted with an experimental Lawrencetune hardtop that was eventually marketed to Morgan owners.

Le Mans 24 Hour race, 1962. Chris Lawrence takes the chequered flag, finishing first in the 2 litre Grand Touring Car class at an average speed of 94 mph.

Peter Morgan negotiates one of the off-road sections of a trials event in the prototype Plus 4 Plus. His son
Charles Morgan was the navigator.

Cyril Charlesworth tackles Tillerton in the 1964 Exeter Trial.

Mrs Pauline Cooper waits her turn in her 1957 Plus 4 at the start of a London Motor Club Rally, late 1950s.

Ray Meredith leads the pack through Copse Corner at Silverstone in his Morgan Plus 4 on 15 April 1963. He finished third.

Peter Morgan strives to maintain adhesion and motion in his 4/4 in the MMEC Shenstone/Morgan Sports Car Club's Production Car Trial in March 1963. The passenger is Mrs Jane Morgan.

Morgans excelled in rallies and trials events. Here one of them takes 'Stretes' in the 1964 Exeter Trial at speed.

Ruth Atkinson from Swansea became a very accomplished and successful rally and trials driver during the early 1970s. Rallies were not just daytime events as can clearly be seen in the photograph above.

Morganeering has always been a family activity. In this photograph Ruth Atkinson's car is being driven by her husband in the Penrice Hill climb in 1971. In this event the car was used by the whole family with remarkable success. In all they took the following awards: Best Lady, Best over 40 (Ruth's husband), Best 1600 unmodified (her eldest son) and the best non-car driver (ex-motorcyclist – her younger son Peter, who was fastest of them all).

Ruth succumbed to cancer, but her exploits and memory live on through the Ruth Atkinson Trophy which is presented each year by the Morgan Sports Car Club for the best performance by a member driving a Morgan in the MCC Trials, Exeter, Lands End and Edinburgh.

Cyril Charlesworth, with his wife Joyce as 'bouncer', tackles 'Blue Hills Mine' in the 1975 MCC Lands End Trial.

Peter Askew in his Lightweight Plus 8 leads the way through a corner at Silverstone.

The prototype Plus 8 (note the two bumps on the bonnet) driven by Bill Fink, the USA west coast Morgan agent, takes the chequered flag in a race in America after the car had eventually been sold by the factory.

Not all trials courses are mud all the time. Here Barry Sumner and John Timms wait to start the next section of the Exeter Trial in 1985. The temperatures were exceptionally low that year, in fact the coldest in modern times, and the course was rock hard. The Morgan immediately behind Barry Sumner is the pre-war specially designed factory short chassis Trials 4-4 owned by Roger Comber.

Peter Askew in his specially prepared 4/4, competing in the Bentley Drivers' Club Morgan-only race at Silverstone in 1988. He finished sixth overall, being the first 4/4 home behind the big Plus 8s.

Barry Sumner and John Timms in Barry's 1650 cc 4/4 on the way to a Gold Award in the 1987 MCC Edinburgh Trial. 1987 saw him win Gold Awards in the two other MCC trials events, Exeter and Lands End, culminating in a coveted Triple Award, the first to be won by a Morgan for some twenty years. They also won the Baddley Award for the best performance by any car in that year's trials.

Britain's first ever continuous 24-hour motor race was held at Snetterton, June 21/22 1980. In all five Morgans were entered. One of these was a single entry from Morris Stapleton Motors and had a four-driver crew of Bruce Stapleton, Bill Wykeham, Richard Down and John Spero. The car was in fact Vivien Morgan's shopping car and it enjoyed trouble-free racing, covering 1732.97 miles and winning the coveted Commander's Cup for the greatest distance covered by a single car entry.

One of the most competitive Morgan owners in America is John H. Shealy II. He is seen here taking the chequered flag in his Modsports Morgan winning the D-Modified race at Southside Speedway in July 1987.

He is seen here again winning his race, at the same race track, this time in his A-Stock Morgan Plus 8, in 1996.

Peter Askew leads the pack at 'Bridge' corner at Silverstone in the Morgan only race at the Bentley Drivers' Club meeting on 29 August 1987 in his highly modified 4/4. He finished fourth overall behind three Plus 8s.

MCC Lands End Trial, 1988. Barry Sumner and Rick Bourse attack the classic Crackington Hill.

Kent Forest Stages Event. Barry Sumner and Keith Morris in Jan Sumner's 1953 Plus 4, which finished a staggering first overall on the demanding forest stage event. Interestingly the stage times posted by the Plus 4 put it well within the top six modern rally car event.

Monte Carlo Rally, 1991. Barry Sumner and Keith Morris again in Jan Sumner's 1953 Plus 4. They started from Edinburgh and endured snow and ice throughout the week-long event together with temperatures of -30 degrees C throughout France, all without a hood. They finished first in class and sixth overall.

Barry Sumner and Pam Durham awaiting the start of the London to Sydney rally at Chelsea Harbour, London, 17 April 1993. They crossed twelve countries in thirty days. The Morgan was the oldest car in the event. Below, they await the start of a street stage of the same rally in Kalgoorlie, Australia.

Morgans are enjoyed by all the family no matter how many years apart. In the top photograph Ray Meredith tackles Prescott hill climb in 1960. Below, his son Michael is at the same location in a more modern car in 1996.

The 1996 works race car being driven by Charles Morgan at speed. The project was to develop and race prove a car which can be entered in the 24 Hour Le Mans race. Chris Lawrence of 1962 Le Mans and Lawrencetune fame has been called in to work alongside Charles Morgan on the project. © Sutton Motor Sport Images.

The 1997 works race car, chassis number SA9P8400004R11710. This is the first all aluminium coachbuilt Morgan, seen here at its first race outing, at Silverstone, May 1997. © Sutton Motor Sport Images.

# ACKNOWLEDGEMENTS

No book of this type can be compiled without the unstinted co-operation of many people.

Firstly I must once again record my sincere thanks to Peter Morgan, Charles Morgan and the staff of the Morgan Motor Company for yet again giving me their unfailing assistance, with provision of works photographs and a mass of material from their archives.

I also wish to offer my sincere thanks to all those other people who were so ready to assist in the compiling of this photographic record of the Morgan Motor Company and their products over the years. In alphabetical order they are: Aerofilms, Peter Askew, Peter Atkinson, Cliff Baker, Ken Bayliss, John Bone, Gregory Huston-Bowden, Mrs Mary Chapman (Colin Chapman), Mrs Pauline Cooper, Colin Cruddas (Cobham PLC), Mike Duncan, Miss June Hebden (Malvern Museum), Michael and Ray Meredith, Roger Richmond, Mrs Pam Roberts, Craig Schubert, J.A. Slade, John H. Sheally II, Barry Sumner, Paul Sutton (Sutton Motor Sport Images), Richard Tipping, Ted Walker (Harold Baker), J. Willburn.

I have obtained many of these photographs from those left to me by the late Dick Pritchard, which he had collected over a period of forty years or more; the exact origin of these photographs is unknown. I know that he assembled material from most motoring magazines including *Light Car & Cyclecar*, *Motor Cycle*, *Motor Cycling*, *Autosport*, *Motor Sport*, *Motor* and *Autocar*, all of which he read regularly. In addition I have collected information and photographs over the past thirty years from magazines, Morgan clubs and Morgan owners from all over the world. In many cases it is now impossible to establish the exact source of certain items, and I therefore offer my heartfelt thanks to all such writers, magazines and photographers.